THE FIVE STAGES OF GROWTH

Lester Young Jr.

Copyright © 2020 Lester Young Jr.

"THE FIVE STAGES OF GROWTH"

Lester Young Jr.

ISBN: 9798671105049
Imprint: Independently published

For more information on Lester Young and his organization, visit Path2Redemption.org

The Five Stages of Growth

Table of Contents

DEDICATION   1

ACKNOWLEDGMENTS   6

INTRODUCTION   9

HEALING FROM HURT   12

FINDING MY VOICE   22

MINDSET   32

DISCOVERING PURPOSE   41

HAVING A VISION   53

DEDICATION

Growing up, my father instilled the power of prayer and the understanding that God existed within our household daily. After my mother passed, I witnessed his faith increase tremendously as he made the adjustment to now being a single parent. I am sure there were times when he was pressured, stressed, or even angry that he is now raising 4 children alone, but he did everything within his soul to make sure my sister's and I were taken care of.

In the months following my mother's death, he attended church services on a regular basis. He became one of the deacons and made himself readily available to helping with whatever was needed for the church to operate smoothly. Naturally, one of the many problem's teenagers face is waking up early on the weekends. Especially on Sunday mornings. Now that dad took on the task of driving the Sunday School Bus, we had no choice but to get up and be ready by the time he pulled up in the yard.

Having arguments or disagreements became normal during my adolescent years. The one memory that sticks out is the first time I saw disappointment on dad's face. It was after I was caught selling drugs in school and he met me at the detention center. I knew he was devastated. We rode home in complete silence. Once we were settled in, he said to me... "Son, why are you doing this"? I held my head down and replied... "I don't know". A few days had passed, and yet my dad still seem down and bothered.

Even though he had told me time and time again what could happen if I did not change, the day I was sentenced to prison was another day of disappointment mixed with hurt. As time passed, our bond grew stronger. It was his words of wisdom that got me through 22 years of prison. What he shared with me more than anything was that "prayer is the best medicine". Despite the distance, he and my sisters remained faithful to our visits. I am not sure who's smile was more contagious, mind when I saw him or his when he saw me. Nevertheless, I knew he loved me, and I was determined to make him proud.

His support during my incarceration was steady and consistent. Seeing him sitting across the courtroom as I stood before the parole board gave me strength. As I spoke with determination, confidence, and purpose, I saw tears fall from his eyes and his smile was brighter than the sun. I knew he was impressed with how well I represented myself before the board. Within minutes of my deliverance, he had a huge sigh of relief when the clerk came to the door and said... "Mr. Young, you have been approved for parole". Hearing him say... "Son, I always knew you had this in you, I am so proud of the man that you become", made my heart smile. I was blessed to be given a second chance to continue doing all that I could to keep a smile on his face and give him more and more reasons to be proud.

On August 2, 2020; the sunset on my best friend. Nothing could have EVER prepared me for that phone call I received from my sister that the "anchor" of our family had passed away. Still on this very day replaying those words shakes my soul.

As children, we hope and pray that our parents live forever, but that is not how we were created. Having knowledge of God and understanding the power of prayer is what keeps my family and I strong. Dad dedicated his life to serving God by being the best example of a "God-fearing" man that walked by faith.

Looking back on the past 6 years of being home, I am certain that his life's lessons groomed my stages of growth. From him I learned how to heal from hurt, through his wisdom I found my voice, his positive attitude motivated the shift within my mindset, his daily agenda helped me to discover my purpose, and his faith in prayer helped in molding the vision for my future.

I will forever cherish our daily talks, and the advice he shared about living a life filled with "no regrets". I am happy knowing that up until his last day, my dad always ended every phone call with saying … "Son, I love you and I'm very proud of you". I will continue making you proud dad!!

IN LOVING MEMORY OF DEACON LESTER YOUNG SR.

JANUARY 13, 1950-AUGUST 2, 2020

"Thank you for being a great example of love, strength, and wisdom. We will continue to celebrate and cherish your legacy. Rest well Pops... Job well done."

~Your children, grandchildren, great-grandchildren

ACKNOWLEDGEMENTS

If nothing else, my journey in life thus far has proven that when you acknowledge, believe in, and praise God during the good and the bad times, anything is possible!

I am honored and blessed to have my best friend and wife Felicia by my side! The strength and resilience she has displayed from day one has been and STILL remains phenomenal! She invested in me, believed in me, and NEVER allowed me to give up. Our bond continues growing with every day that passes, and I promise to do everything within my power to keep that smile on your face! You are indeed one to the best blessings! I love you always!

Knowing that my legacy will continue to live on with and through my 5-year-old daughter Kaleeyah, is a constant reminder to remain consistent in my beliefs, and faithful in my actions. This little girl lives up to the meaning of her name, "most bright, intelligent, beautiful one". Her personality enlightens every room she enters, and she is blessed with a heart of gold. If God wills, and life lasts, I promise to instill the same morals and values within you that my parents instilled within me. Daddy loves you baby girl!

My sisters are the perfect examples of "Roses that grew from concrete". Those that were there and witnessed our journey would agree that these ladies are truly the "Most Valuable Players" when it comes to rising above barriers and maintaining the bond of family. I know our parents are overwhelmed with happiness and joy. Tracey, my prayer is that God continues blessing you for stepping up and keeping the family intact after the demise of our mother. Despite life's obstacles, you stood firm, held your head high, and NEVER allowed anything to break your spirits. Suzette, your motivation for greatness continues inspiring me. It is a pleasure watching as you continue pursuing your dreams of evolving into your own boss. Evelina, the past couple of years sitting with you, talking with you, and learning from you have been blissful. You set your goals and did not allow anything to deter you from achieving them. I have watched you sacrifice a lot in order to be where you are today.

Continue being the best that you can be and always know that your big brother is only a phone call away. Words will never fully express the pure and genuine love I will always have for each of you!

Speaking against criminal reform and helping those formerly incarcerated is personal for me. Not many people can say they get paid to do what they enjoy. To my family at JUSTLEADERSHIPUSA, I will forever be indebted to you for allowing me the opportunity to be a part of your organization. I look forward too many more years of passing ordinances and opening doors for those returning to home from prison.

Thanks to everyone that continues believing in me and investing in my dreams!

INTRODUCTION

For those that have known me since I was a teenager, one could easily recognize that the man that stands before them today has changed. Some view incarceration as a "bad place" or as an institution in which "bad people" are held. To a certain extinct, that could be an accurate way of describing incarceration. As for me, I was able to learn, reprogram my mindset, and grow from issues I was afraid to acknowledge.

Being a mentor, class instructor, and a teacher of religion changed my overall prospective of the future. With so much going on, I was surprised to receive a letter from The Department of Probation that a date had been set for me to appear before the board for my second chance at parole. I pride myself on the fact that not only had I prepared psychologically, mentally, and emotionally for this day; I also envisioned the outcome of the parole board. While waiting to appear before the board, I rehearsed how I was going to convince 7 board members that I should be granted parole. Twenty-two years had passed, and I was NOT the immature, disrespectful, wayward teenager I was when the judge sentenced me to serve a 20- year life sentence. After 5 minutes of presenting my case, and showing each member how I had changed, the decision of parole was granted.

As I ran to the car in the rain, I carried a box of things I chose to not only remind me of my journey but encourage me of my promise to be a better me. I have always heard that my life was not going to be much of anything, only a reflection of my friends and environment. Hearing this conjured up the fighting spirit within to defeat old habits of thinking and seeing my life in a different perspective. While incarcerated, my life's purpose had been revealed. I saw visions of personally and professionally mentoring individuals on a path of change by using my own experiences as a reference point. It is important to know and understand before your demise why God placed you exactly where you are and to whom your message is meant to be shared with. I am certain that I will not revert to the lifestyle I thought to be good for me while I was a teenager. I am thankful for the journey, but my path has indeed taken a different course.

Prison was my institution of higher education. I grew mentally, spiritually, and emotionally. I faced obstacles that challenged finding my purpose, shifting my mindset, reclaiming my voice, having a vision, and healing from my hurt. Despite the journey, the razor wire fences, and the 20 years that had to be served BEFORE being eligible for parole, I never stopped believing that all things were possible. I continued working to better myself daily by shaping my behavior and choosing a positive path of redemption. Thus far, since being released my journey has been phenomenal. I look forward to continuing to walk in areas that I only thought I would see in my dreams.

HEALING FROM HURT

"If you never heal from what hurt you, you'll bleed on people who didn't cut you".

~Klara Burke

"Hurt people hurt others because they themselves have been hurt". This statement speaks volumes in truth. Each of us has experienced hurt to one degree or another. Some people can process pain, heal from it, then move on, while others are severely damaged. This can cause an individual to become defensive or angry, which makes others more accessible to become targets of their wrath.

For many years, I suffered with denial, and feelings of brokenness. Therefore, hurting people because I was hurting was easily justified by my actions. After living this way for so long, I assumed this to be normal. Many people find peace within a bottle of alcohol or picking up drugs to temporarily soothe their pain. Luckily, I was smart enough to comprehend that these were only temporary solutions. Sure, for a few hours or so you will be able to rest or experience whatever happiness you feel you are lacking, but eventually it wears off and that hurt comes right back into full effect. Drinking was not my forte, but I did smoke marijuana to ease my thoughts. I adapted the motto that I would hold everything that bothers me within. That way, I only dealt with it privately.

The day before I was arrested, I had an eerie feeling. Almost as if I knew something was about to happen, I just did not understand what it could be. For the first time since burying my mother, I finally built up the courage to visit her grave. For months, I had dreams about her, I knew this was her way of preparing me for what was about to happen. Walking up to the gravesite, I reflected to my childhood days. Mom always made me feel better just by extending her arms out for me to embrace her in a hug. Now more than ever, I wanted to feel my mother's arms wrapped around me. I wanted to hear her say… "Son, everything is going to be just fine". This time, I knew things would NOT be fine. As tears filled my eyes, I could not stop thinking that once again, I had let my mother down. Not to mention, as a result of my actions, someone had lost their life. I was indeed in the worst state of depression.

Shortly after my arrest, the thoughts of suicide surfaced. The more days passed, the more frequently I entertained this notion. I was not at all ready to face the consequences of my actions. How was I going to spend the rest of my life in prison? In my mind, the best way to do this was an overdose of pills. I began complaining to the nurse in the county jail about having bad headaches. She gave me pills. I continued doing this daily until I had accumulated roughly 50 to 70 pills. The time had come to make the attempt. Owning up to the actions of my consequences were becoming harder to accept.

Out of all the men there, God hand-picked this guy to be my roommate. For some reason, he just would NOT stop talking to me. As he continued talking, I laid there patiently waiting him out so that I could end this pain, suffering, and depression. He found every little thing to engage in a conversation. My roommate was a recovering drug addict. I know this because I had sold drugs to him on a few occasions. Lots of time had passed and his mind was much clearer. He was not the same man as he was in the streets. Still, I could not understand the reasoning behind the excessive talking. Finally, after much idle chitter chatter, he looked at me and said... "Young brother, since the day you came into this cell, you have not talked much, nor have you been eating. I have noticed you asking for pills from the nurses every time they come by. I don't know what's on your mind, but

whatever it is, God will take care of it."
Hearing those words sent chills straight to my
soul in ways I had never experienced before.
The tears flowed. They flowed exactly as they
did that day that I visited my mom's grave,
only this time, I felt relief. The pain,
loneliness, and brokenness were NO longer
weighing heavily in my heart. As hard as I
appeared to be, I was not bothered that this
man stood there watching me cry. All he said
was "crying is good, it's the beginning of
healing". You never know who God *"will
come through to relay a message to you"*.
Given this man's past and knowing the details
of what this night was supposed to be, I know
God was using this man to get his message to
me. He went on encouraging me to give God
a second chance at turning this situation
around, and to NOT take those pills or
anything else I may had been putting aside for
this attempt. He introduced me to Islam, and
the teachings of "The Holy Quran". We read
together, we prayed together, then he told
me to kneel and talk to God as if I was in the
cell alone. I did just as he had instructed me
to do. Before it was all over, I remember
laying in the fetal position talking to God

asking forgiveness and strength as I continued dealing with my struggles. I felt a gentle calm come across my body, almost as if God himself had just placed his hands on me and removed my pain. I reached under my pillow, grabbed the pills, walked over to the toilet, and watched as they swirled around the bowl of the toilet then disappeared. Just like that, I was ready to take his advice to give God a second chance, and this time, allow him to lead my steps.

Walking around my neighborhood, I often heard the elder men within the community say, "Men don't cry". This made sense to me because until the day I was paroled, I never saw my father cry. Being that "men" were saying this, you would think it was a true statement. Even at my mother's funeral, dad remained calm and did not shed a tear. Of course, he was hurting! I guess being our strength was more important than succumbing to his own grief. Nonetheless, not seeing him cry only gave fuel to the words of the elders. This added to my pain and damaged me more than the hurt I was carrying.

Emotional Processing is the ability to acknowledge and identify the pain of extreme events. You work to develop a plan of action that helps remove past underlying hurt that continues to linger. Finding excuses not to emotionally process pain is a part of our human condition. By denying, or dishonoring your authentic self, your body slips into an emotional suffering. Naturally with change you should expect a battle between the "old" and the 'new" you. It is a struggle when dismissing the old, and adopting the new, but feeling joy, and happiness enter back into your life is like watching the sun rise. It is peaceful, soothing, provides a calm presence, and begins the journey of a new day.

I knew I had to change something. I was still telling myself I was alright by pushing my emotions to the side. Unless you have experienced this, an individual will fully never understand how holding on to a broken spirit and resisting the urge to ask for help can greatly impact the choices that are made within your everyday life. I had decided it was time to begin addressing past hurt, rejections, and anger. I could not ignore the healing that was needed to mend my inner wounds. In order to move on I had to begin processing the pain that was necessary to heal the hurt. I thought back to the cry I shared with my roommate. Releasing pain through my tears felt good and empowering. As those tears rolled down my cheeks, I could breathe. The process of healing had begun.

God works in mysterious ways. A few days later, my roommate was transferred. I was deeply saddened to see him leave. While walking out of the cell, he said... "Allah (God) allowed our paths to cross for many reasons". He and I both agreed that our talk was a part of his plan. Little did I know the man I had once sold drugs to NOT ONLY saved me from attempting suicide but would be the one to physically provide me with the spiritual blueprint that I so desperately needed to heal.

I am not proud of the circumstances that bought about the hurt and pain I carried. It was self-inflicted. Daily I grieve for the actions that came about as a result of my negligence and lack of concern for myself or others. Processing not only meant seeking forgiveness for my actions but forgiving myself and slowly begin to put the pieces of my life together. This began the night I opened myself up to God, making peace with my mother's passing, and the soul of my victim. Coming to terms with these 3 things changed my prospective. I was able to breathe. I was no longer suppressing my emotions. Instead of being the guy hurting people because I was hurt, I became the guy wanting to heal those still battling with their own emotional pain.

Despite all the negative talk, influences, and behaviors, I was able to heal in prison. Asking for forgiveness, then forgiving myself was a key component. Daily looking into the mirror, loving the glow of prosperity from the reflection looking back at me, speaking positive affirmations, and removing myself from negative people gave me the confidence needed to walk away from feelings of low self-esteem. Reciting affirmations gave me purpose and shifted my mindset. Power is in your words, so be careful of what you speak into existence.

The following are affirmations I recited daily:

1. You are a gift from God.
2. I love everything about myself.
3. You have a purpose.
4. God is preparing you for greatness.
5. Love the reflection from the face looking back at you in the mirror.
6. I am smart, intelligent, and incredibly handsome.
7. Your mistakes do not define your future.
8. You are worthy of God's blessings overflowing in your life.

FINDING MY VOICE

"It's not about finding your voice; it's about giving yourself permission to use your voice."

~Kriss Carr

Immediately after a baby enters the world, their voice is heard. Until the baby can speak, the tone of their voice helps parents understand exactly what is needed. It allows an individual to have the ability to influence outcomes and creates a personal connection between people. Your voice is an instrument, a natural expression of who you are and a way to be heard. It carries with it the story of life, a spectrum that can range from joyous to difficult. It reflects your views, thoughts, and feelings.

Growing up I suffered with lots of insecurities. My appearance was not appealing, my clothes were not up to par with my peers, and I was not as smart as I could have been. When asked to read aloud by my teachers, I was embarrassed. Not only because I disliked my voice but reading or speaking to my peers was intimidating. In my mind, it was easier for me to have friends by just being who they wanted me to be, saying what they wanted me to say, and naturally doing what they wanted me to do.

I was 16 when my mother passed away. This was a trying time in my life. Mom kept the foundation strong. She taught my sisters and me the importance of speaking up for ourselves. Every morning before we left home for school, she shared words of encouragement then sent us off to have a great day. The day she died is the day I lost my "voice". I shut down. I had no clue how to process my thoughts or articulate to anyone my emotions. Mom was the glue to the family. She was the one that made everything right and was always there for me to talk with. Now that she was gone, I struggled with finding someone to confide in. Therefore, turning to selling drugs and smoking marijuana was my "way out".

Mentally, I was messed up and had convinced myself that the only way I could cope with this pain, this grief, and this loss was to hide it deep down within, put on a tough face and do what I did best, be what others wanted me to be.

Can you imagine the anxiety I felt sitting in a court room at the age of 19 facing a murder charge? I listened as different people testified by stating the events they remembered from that night. It seems as if each testimony, was different from the last. Some lied, some told the truth. Nevertheless, I sat there, calm with a smirk on my face. My arrogance convinced me that I would walk away from this. At this pivotal time in my life, my only concern was not showing a sign of weakness. I refused to show my friends that I was afraid. When it was my time to testify, the time set aside for me to tell the truth as to what happened, I did the opposite of what my mother taught me to do. Instead of using my voice to speak up for myself, I simply sat there and said "nothing". During the trial, I sat in silence. The solicitor, and witnesses painted a picture to the jury of an awful person. I knew this was not true, I knew this was not me, but lacking my voice made it impossible to defend myself.

A few hours had passed, and the judge requested the jury's verdict. For 3 days, I sat through this and did not defend myself, nor did anyone testifying speak in my favor. When the jury gave a "guilty" verdict, I was outraged! Instead of blaming myself for the life sentence with eligibility of parole after serving 20 years that the judge issued me, I blamed my lawyer for poor misrepresentation, the solicitor for convincing my friend to testify against me, and everyone that lied on the stand. I was always taught that the power of choices made **"today"** can affect your **"tomorrow"**. Looking back on my teenage years, I made a lot of reckless decisions. The lack of my education, self-esteem, self-worth, and morals were no longer of value.

As I was escorted from the courtroom and placed inside of a holding cell, I sat in silence. I wanted to cry but could not, I wanted to speak, but would not. I held the pain inside and asked myself, "How am I going to do this time?", and "Will I ever see the outside again?". Years later, I realized the reason I was placed in prison had nothing to do with the jury's verdict, the people that testified against me, or the poor misrepresentation of my court appointed attorney. It is your basic "cause" and "effect" law. The **"cause"** of my actions paving my path to prison was the **"effect"** of the judge physically placing me there.

Still not fully accepting responsibility for my actions, I gave up hope of ever seeing the outside of prison. Like many, my father was deeply hurt, embarrassed and bothered by my actions. Despite the situation, he continued praying for me. In every visit, he would apologize for not being more of a positive role model in my life, and how he deeply regretted not providing my siblings and me with more love and attention during and after the passing of our mother. Dad reiterated the importance of me finding my voice. He reminded me of what my mom taught us daily, and how important she stressed to not wallow in self-pity and regret. It was during those moments that I was forced to stop feeling sorry for myself. I felt more and more uplifted with every visit from my dad. When he left his words of encouragement remained in the atmosphere.

Again, to some, prison is a building in which people are legally held as a punishment for a crime they have committed. For me, prison was a university of higher learning and an opportunity to heal. It was what some would say is "hands on experience". Either I was going to sit back and let this time do me in, or take this time to learn, educate, and groom myself to do better. After years of sitting idle, I choose the latter. I adopted 3 strategies to help find my voice:

- Surrounded myself with other like-mind individuals that encouraged me to speak truthfully by healing inwardly.
- When I realized I was shutting down and afraid to use my voice, I learned to lean into my own discomfort and speak my truth.
- I found strength in healing from my past to be able to embrace the future.

One day while speaking to the men incarcerated with me, the chaplain said... "Lester, you're called for something great. I've never seen anyone inside the chapel including myself receive the FULL attention during instruction as you do". My response was... "Chap, it's not hard to speak to anyone when you're speaking from the same pain they carry or have experienced".

Reclaiming my voice felt great. My confidence level increased. My Automatic Negative Thinking was replaced with positive energy. Standing in front of fellow men incarcerated and using my life's experiences to help them overcome their own insecurities and triggers was what I vowed to continue doing for as long as God willed me to do so. With each talk, my voice lifted higher and higher. Almost as if it were demanding attention, demanding to be heard. Hearing my voice speak positive into others made me happy. I had found my voice while serving time. I have always said..." the thing you want the most could be the worst thing for you, and the thing you don't want at all is usually the best thing to ever happen to you".

Today I speak with confidence and compassion. All too many times, random people approach me after hearing me speak. I am always humbled while hearing them say how powerful my speech was, and how out of all the speakers, it was the conviction within my voice that demanded their attention the most. At my first youth conference, one of my former teachers surprised me with his attendance. He came up, hugged me, and then said, "You have changed, and had I asked you to speak like that in front of your classmates in middle school you would've found a reason to be dismissed from class. Now look at you... you are speaking in front of 300+ people with no fear, no flinching, and no anxiety... you've found your voice and I'm immensely proud of you!"

Finding my voice while incarcerated prepared me for the lifestyle I lead today. I am an Author, Motivational Speaker, and Certified Transformational Life Coach. Sharing my lived experiences with others enables me to help them unlock their potential. My hope is that everyone makes the choice to use their voice to motivate and be an inspiration for others.

Follow along with exercises to help with finding your voice:

1. How are you using your voice to connect with your purpose?

2. What does your voice reveal about your personality?

3. What areas of uniqueness are you holding back from being revealed in your voice?

4. Is there anything in your life that is causing you to feel a sense of shame?

5. If so, is this preventing you from speaking your truth?

6. Record yourself speaking about a memory that created sadness for you growing up. Listen to this recording daily for one week. At the end of the week, you should have 5 statements reflecting different emotions inflicted by that one memory.

7. Once you have identified with those things that took your voice, purchase 5 balloons. Write each emotion from 1 to 5 on a strip of paper. Tie that paper to the balloon. Recite aloud what you wrote, say a prayer immediately following, then release the balloon into the air as a symbolic release representing that one thing that stole your voice.

MINDSET

"If my mind can CONCEIVE it, and my heart can BELIEVE it-then I can ACHIEVE it".

~Muhammad Ali

I was a prisoner within my mind long before I was sentenced to prison. At the age of 17, I was hanging out in clubs, fighting, and caught selling drugs while at school. Walking across a stage to receive a diploma, and attending college was not a thought in any long-term goals that I had planned for my life. I made careless mistakes, lived reckless, and smoked marijuana all day.

My friends and I had accepted that we were living on borrowed time. We knew eventually our choices would lead to a terrible fate but being in the limelight and reaping the benefits of selling drugs came with a street credit that lots of teenagers craved to have. The music we listened to only reinforced our thinking. Of course, that was a sad way of living, but we all had little education and knew our future consisted of being incarcerated or being deceased by the age of 21. This was our "reality", our "normal", and our everyday "way of life."

For many years I did not see myself as being someone of value nor did I feel that I could be of value to others. This narrative effected my self-esteem, self-worth, confidence, and lack of trust. These insecurities fueled my disrespectful behavior and made it hard to believe that any woman I was involved with could genuinely love me. The lifestyle I lived consisted of multiple women and being true to one just was not the "cool" thing to do.

After I was caught with drugs and arrested at school, I sat in the backseat of the police car in deep thought. For the first time I thought about how many people (including my father) had warned me of this exact moment. My behavior changed from "fierce" to "puzzling" as the police car pulled up to the detention center. My dad was there, but instead of him being angry, and yelling as I was removed from the car, he simply stood there with a troubling look of disappointment. I could deal with him being angry, but disappointed was unfamiliar territory that I never prepared for. After being released on bond, I was able to leave with my dad. That was the longest 45-minute ride home in complete silence.

I was caught with a street value of $1K in drugs, along with $2500 in cash. Being a youthful offender, and this being my first offense, the judge sentenced me to serve 90 days at a military bootcamp. To some, this would be an eye opener. A warning that would scare your average teenager into straightening up and flying right. Not me, being given this time increased my street creditability with my friends and rivals. I counted the days until I would be released to get back into the streets. My mindset convinced me that I had lost too much money and would now have to increase drug sells in order to compensate for the loss of being in bootcamp.

One thing I have learned is God will send warning(s) before destruction. Eighteen months after bootcamp, I was involved in a drug deal that had gone bad. A few days later, I was arrested. Several months later, the jury found me guilty of murder and I was sentenced to a 20-year life sentence and not eligible for parole until 20 years had been served.

Just like that, I had spoken this into existence. I knew my fate would be this or being killed before the age of 21. The thoughts of possibly spending the rest of my life in prison after serving 20 years took a toll on me. Here I was, a big-time drug dealer that never showed fear, nor any emotion to the thought of being killed or incarcerated.

Given warning, after warning, after more warnings, and now that the day had come, my emotions were all over the place. Still, I was not convinced that I needed to change. After witnessing a few fights, and deaths within the first week of my incarceration, I was now focused on surviving. I quickly adapted to what things to do and not to do, as well as whom to entertain and not to entertain.

I signed up to be a part of the religious class out-count. As I was leaving a chaplain asked that I come back to talk with him. During our conversation, he asked about my life, the length of my sentence, and what my 5-year goals were. I responded by stating I had no goals because I have been given a life sentence and will probably never see the real world again. His response was "freedom starts in the mind first, and that can take place even in prison". Before leaving, he suggested that I read a book designed to shape my mindset. It took about a week, and an additional 3 more times of reading to grasp the concept but reading "As a man thinketh" by James Allen introduced me to a shift in my mindset. This one book increased my hunger to read. Instead of passing by, I was now going into the prison library. My areas of focus were books specializing in personal growth, autobiographies, and anything that increased my knowledge of starting a business.

My actions were the reason I was incarcerated, but my mindset caused the thoughts leading to the behavior that bought about the actions of the crime being committed. The more you speak something into existence, the better the probability becomes that it will more than likely take place. The more I read the more I realized that from the time I was caught selling drugs in school up until the day I was arrested, I had already placed myself in prison, mentally by sabotaging my future with negative affirmations. I had "perfect vision" for the first time in understanding the power of thoughts. Now, I saw the need to change.

During my reading, I focused on an exercise that stressed the importance of gratitude. Every morning and every night I wrote in my journal 5 things that I was grateful for on that day. Doing this consistently bought about a positive attitude.

Some nights, I would sit up jotting notes from the book. I was intentional about "unlearning" the bad narratives that played a part in shaping my earlier childhood behaviors. I came across the term "Auto Suggestion". This is the hypnotic or subconscious adoption of an idea that one must originate with through repetition of verbal statements in order to change behavior. This process works by deleting negative thoughts, using positive affirmations, and use of boring repetitive tasks as an opportunity for reprogramming your thoughts.

How to create positive affirmations:

The daily use of positive affirmations interrupts and replaces negative thoughts and beliefs.

To achieve this, you must continuously flood your subconscious with thoughts and images of who you desire to become

When creating your 5 daily affirmations, be sure to include the following key components:

1. Start by using the words "I am". These words are powerful tools when speaking positivity in your life.
2. Make sure to keep your daily affirmations brief, that way it is easier memorize while practicing and reciting.
3. Make your affirmations specific to goals you have set and daily strive to achieve.
4. Be sure your affirmations contain a word that promotes "action."
5. Remember, your affirmations are for you and YOU alone!

Examples:

I am happy and grateful

I am living in abundance

I am so happy and grateful to be able to be living a healthy lifestyle

I am at peace with the being the person God created me to be

Start your gratitude journal:

For the next 60 days, write down 10 different daily affirmations, 5 in the morning and 5 before bed.

THE FIVE STAGES OF GROWTH

In prison, it is remotely easy to convince your mind of the lifestyle you want to lead once you are home. Your view of the world from inside of your cell is NOTHING compared to the complexity of what you will be faced with once you are home. The most difficult lesson I encountered the first few months after being released was fitting my affirmations from prison into my daily tasks of being home. At that moment, it dawned on me that my life was placed on hold and the world continued moving forward in my absence. These months are the most critical as they determine how strong you are to push through.

Having a strong support group and multiple accountability partners kept me centered. The journals filled with notes were reminders of where my life once was and where I vowed it would not be again. I revised my daily affirmations to coincide with new goals and aspirations suitable to making the transition of now being home more manageable.

DISCOVERING PURPOSE

"Instead of trying to build a brick wall, lay a brick everyday…eventually you'll look up and you'll have a brick wall."

~Nipsey Hustle

Purpose guides life decisions, influences behavior, shapes goals, and offers a sense of direction. It is something that gives you pure joy while you are in the act of doing it. When you are not motivated for no other reason than to share your talents, gifts, and experiences with others in hopes of bringing

about change. When you do something
with purpose, you do it with determination.

During my school years, I was not the kid
anyone would vote as "most likely to
succeed" or "most likely to accomplish"
anything. I did not make, nor did I place
myself in any position to receive good grades.
Making an impact, speaking purpose, and
inspiring others, was not at all any label
someone would attach to me. So, here I am,
19 years old, sitting in the Department of
Corrections, with a sentence longer than I had
been in society. Trying to wrap my head
around the fact that I would possibly spend
the rest of my life inside of prison. Imagine
my surprise the day I realized my life had
meaning and that there was a reason for
everything that happened. Never in a
thousand years could I EVER HAD pictured that
during my darkest days GOD would reveal his
purpose for my life.

Allen Young Sr., (my dad's oldest brother)
was serving life in a Boston prison. I would say
around this time, Uncle Allen had already
been in prison 5-6 years prior to me. He was a

devoted Christian and highly respected in prison for teaching others the word of GOD. He and my aunt printed monthly Christian newsletters that circulated not only through the prison system, but to his church family as well. After conversing through letters and visits with my dad, he decided to write me a letter. Despite his situation, he remained calm, by holding on to the words he taught others that promised the mercy, favors, and blessings of God. His faith was extraordinarily strong. My uncle was the perfect example of turning his pain into his purpose. Every month I received a newsletter from him. I noticed with every letter; his "positivity" always found a way to motivate a change within me. After a while I NO longer viewed his letters as mail, this to me was his way of personally sending a piece of himself to me via pen and paper!

We continued writing back and forth for years. Out of all his letters, one spoke directly to me. He said, *"pain reveals you to yourself, and your reason for being created by God will be revealed"*. I paced the floor for a while, replaying what I had just read. I realized that my own personal pain and adversities were molding me to become a man I never believed existed within me. Once I acknowledged this, I also realized I was becoming my uncle. I mentioned earlier feeling as though he was sending a piece of himself to me with each letter. I was experiencing a spiritual connection. I was undergoing prayer, and fasting, as well as studying the word of God. I found strength in being positive, and strength in seeking spiritual guidance.

Little did he know, his words helped with the shifting of my mindset. My negative demeanor for so long allowed me to view my sentence as punishment. His letters, and words helped me realize that my sentence was a blessing in which God was grooming me to become a better "me". I stopped asking God "why am I here" and started asking God to "please allow me to learn from this painful situation". My purpose had been revealed and became clear to me to teach from my experiences in hopes of helping others prevent taking the same path. I began sitting, talking, mentoring, and teaching the men incarcerated with me. I used my **own** fears, triggers, feelings of brokenness, and emotions to not only build my self-confidence and self-worth, but to help them realize their own potential of growing from old habits as well. Now, waking up in prison came with an agenda, and that was to make the day count for something greater than me.

I was studying one day in the prison library with a friend. He discussed the acronym A.N.T. (Automatic Negative Thinking). The significance in this compared to "ants" is as follows:

> ➢ *Like ants, negativity starts slowly crawling on you, you do not notice it at first, so it continues to crawl, you know it is there but cannot pinpoint the exact location, suddenly you begin to feel the bite**

Sometimes, it is natural to feel a "small hint" of negativity. We naturally have fears, experience lost, encounter some forms of brokenness, and feel alone. Reading the word of God taught me that everyone has experienced adversity. Are you familiar with Job? He suffered what some would assume to be a "huge loss". He did not allow the bite from the A.N.T. to deter him. With faith, prayer, patience, and perseverance, God replaced everything he lost with things better than he had ever imagined were possible. The story of Job is a great affirmation of using your pain to find your purpose. I knew from reading that I had to take control of the "crawling ant". Daily, I began reciting affirmations of God having a great plan for my life, and how he NEVER places a burden upon you in which you DO NOT have the strength to bare". This is how I began (and currently begin) my day. Learning to trust in God's process and timing is KEY.

Always remember, *"While being hit with adversities, you must realize it's important that you do not focus on the "adversity", and DO NOT allow yourself to reminisce on the things you've lost in the process. If you worry about the "adversity", then you'll prolong your growth of moving forward during your moments of darkness, despair, and pain".*

Adversity comes into our lives to shape us and NOT destroy us. The quicker we realize this the better our response is to the challenges of life.

Finding your purpose in life is the one thing that adds value to who you are and why you were created. By listening to what others say about you, you will learn how your purpose impacts their lives as well. When I mixed my experiences with genuinely helping others find their own talents my purpose from my pain was revealed. We all go through circumstances in life that help better the choices for others.

A year after I was released, I founded a 501 (c3) non-profit organization and named it after the programs I taught in prison. "Path2Redemption" provides aftercare assistance to those returning home from prison in their transition back to society after incarceration. The organization also provides mentoring services for at-risk youth, in hopes of preventing them from entering through the pipeline to prison. I remember seeing the "so-called" toughest of the tough enter prison and being the first to break. Seeing this inspired me to work on fulfilling my purpose of being an advocate for youth by supporting and making sure their dreams consisted of walking the floors of colleges or universities instead of prison.

My job has been extremely beneficial in placing me in different platforms in which change is needed and being implemented. I have been able to assist with helping those that are formerly incarcerated and have felony convictions with being considered for job opportunities by having a "Ban the Box" ordinance passed with 5 counties located within South Carolina. Now these individuals have better opportunities of employment within different cities and counties across South Carolina.

In 2019, I was invited to Washington, DC, by an organization that advocates for higher education for those incarcerated. I was asked to share my story with the Senators of SC in hopes of having Pell Grants restored within prisons across the country. I walked the halls of "The House of Representatives" with pride and confidence. I knew I was supposed to be there. I thought back to something a friend shared with me in prison. He said... *"your gift will make room for you and place you before great people"*. Once I returned home, I text him immediately letting him know about my experiences in Washington, DC, and how his words uplifted and empowered me.

In fact, whenever I am in a room that I feel an individual that has **served 22 years in prison is NOT supposed to be a part of**, I am reminded that "my gift has placed me before great people". Even though he spoke those words to me over 10 years ago, they continue inspiring me to overcome barriers that I once placed upon myself.

Later that same year, I was invited to attend the 3-day event on Criminal Justice Reform. Being a member of "The 20/20 Bipartisan Organization", I had the pleasure of meeting and individually discussing issues of prison reform with The Democratic Presidential Candidates.

On September 17, 2020; I was granted a full pardon from The South Carolina Board. My rights have been reinstated and one of those rights allows me the opportunity to vote. The recent Presidential Election was my first time exercising my right to vote. Having this right inspires me to educate others on the right of voting and encouraging them to be a part of the voting process on the local and national level.

Follow along with exercises to help with finding your purpose:

1. Are you praying in hopes of learning from your pain?

   _____

2. **What is your purpose in life?**

   _____

   _____

3. List 3 things you have learned from a time in your life.
   a)
   b)
   c)

4. From question 3, list how those 3 situations can help someone else.
   a)
   b)
   c)
5. How are you controlling the A.N.T. in your life?

   _____
   _____
   _____
   _____

6. Using the table below, on a separate sheet of paper, list your pain in the 1st column, then the lessons learned as a result of the pain in the 2nd column.

PAIN	LESSON LEARNED FROM THE PAIN

HAVING A VISION

"The future belongs to those that prepare for it today."

~Malcolm X

A clear vision enables you to see everything differently. It is the most important mental picture that brings your world into focus. Vision can be your personal "why" or be a set of dreams and long-term goals. When having a guide for creating plans it brings order to chaos.

For many, having a vision is all you need! That you wait for it to manifest and DO NOTHING in the process to nurture it. This statement is false. After having the vision, you must invest the work of nurturing it before the manifestation will come to light. I accredit the words and wisdom of an incredibly good friend who introduced me to three principles. "Having a VISION consists of going into the VALLEY before you receive the VICTORY."

My vision started while incarcerated. I dreamed of the day I would be released, the day I would get married, and day I would become a father. This one thought was all I needed to continue being motivated to build and plan. In 1996, I wrote in my journal my parole date which was not scheduled until 2012. Even though I was still facing 16 years, I wanted to continue doing something positive to remain focused on my vision and NOT allow anything cause me to stray. During my time at Allendale Institution, I received information on how to obtain my G.E.D., and decided it was time to take the first step. Once you acknowledge and begin to apply the necessary change within your life, the voice of doubt surfaces. While attending the night classes for my G.E.D., I was asked why I felt the need to take this course knowing I had a life sentence? Had it not been for my shift in mindset, I would have given in and allowed those words to continue planting seeds of doubt inside of my thoughts to prevent growth. I stood firm, remained confident, and refused to allow the projected fears of others live vicariously through my actions. Being led by my vision, I walked away from that conversation with a feeling of empowerment.

My valleys came with many trials. The environment of prison is crowded with individuals that do not have a plan, nor a desire to have a vision. The conversations were filled with despair, the aura was hopeless, and the lack of motivation placed limitations on anyone desiring any type of growth. To have hope in prison was just something you were not encouraged to do. Constantly, you were led to believe that having a vision outside of prison would only end in disappointment. I temporarily gave into this disappointment when I was denied parole in 2012. This rejection hurt deeply and was difficult to accept. I invested lots of time into making sure I would make it on the first try. It is important that you do not confuse a valley with a victory. Sometimes a valley can trick your mind into seeing something as a victory. It allows you to remove ALL obstacles, and it allows you to not prepare for rejection. Some people allow the perception of these valleys to cause them to give up and pull back. Instead of reverting into a state of depression, use this tool for what it was designed to do... motivate you to try harder, encourage you to work smarter, and inspire you to push harder.

My victories came in small wins. Once transferred to Kershaw Correctional Institution, I accepted a job posting to help the prison chaplain. This was not only an opportunity to earn wages, but it was also the perfect piece to add to my portfolio of change. As the chaplain's assistant, my role was to create programs to teach the men incarcerated along with me the skills needed to adapt in society once released. As I prepared for my second parole hearing, I wrote out my purpose plan for my life after prison. In 2014, after strategically planning and rehearsing how I would present myself for the second time, I was granted parole.

The visions of getting married, becoming a father, purchasing a home for my family, starting two businesses, (Path2Redemption, a nonprofit organization from programs I created in prison, and Young's Integrity Pressure Washing), and now being the author of two books are my celebrated victories after passing through the valleys designed to break me!

I understand that moving forward my vision will come with deeper valleys. However, my faith has increased, and with God's lead, I am confident in my steps. Meaning my upcoming victories will produce even greater results.

EXERCISES FOR VISION

1. Write down your vision for the next 5 years for your personal growth, financial status, professional growth, and family.

2. A vision statement is a written document that describes what you want to accomplish in your life both personal and professional.

    a. What is your vision statement?

    b. How does that statement apply to the visions you have listed for question #1?

3. Create a vision board that outlines your goals with pictures you personally chose and cut out from magazines that perfectly identifies with what you are wanting to accomplish.

4. Enlist an accountability partner(s) that you know will hold you accountable to

your goals and deadlines of achieving each goal.

5. Remember to place a checkmark on each picture and add a date that shows that task has been completed.

In loving memory of
Allen Young Sr.

July 1, 1939 – December 18, 2012

"A dream written down with a date becomes a goal, broken down into steps, becomes a plan backed by action becomes a reality".
~Greg Reid

Made in United States
North Haven, CT
16 February 2022

16167528R00038